# INTERNATIONAL ACES

## Volume 2

D1825452

# CHRIS GEARY

# Pilot Memo

International Aces captures the true stories of the world's first great fighter pilots.

Each story is based on carefully researched historical events. Of course, all story-telling is subjective and reflects a partial view of what really happened.

This series has taken nearly four years to complete. Artwork is first drawn in pencil, then brought to life with Ink. Each page is scanned into the computer to be lettered and formatted to create the final Graphic Novel.

Independently created to commemorate 100 years since the First World War, we hope you find these true stories informative and inspiring.

International Aces. The action starts here...

 InkShot.com

International Aces: Volume 2

Published by InkShot.com - creative division of STLwww Ltd
Please contact us at: Aces@InkShot.com
or visit us at: www.InkShot.com

First Edition: December 2012
ISBN 978-1-909199-01-9

# INTERNATIONAL ACES

## Volume 2

# FIRST WORLD WAR SERIES

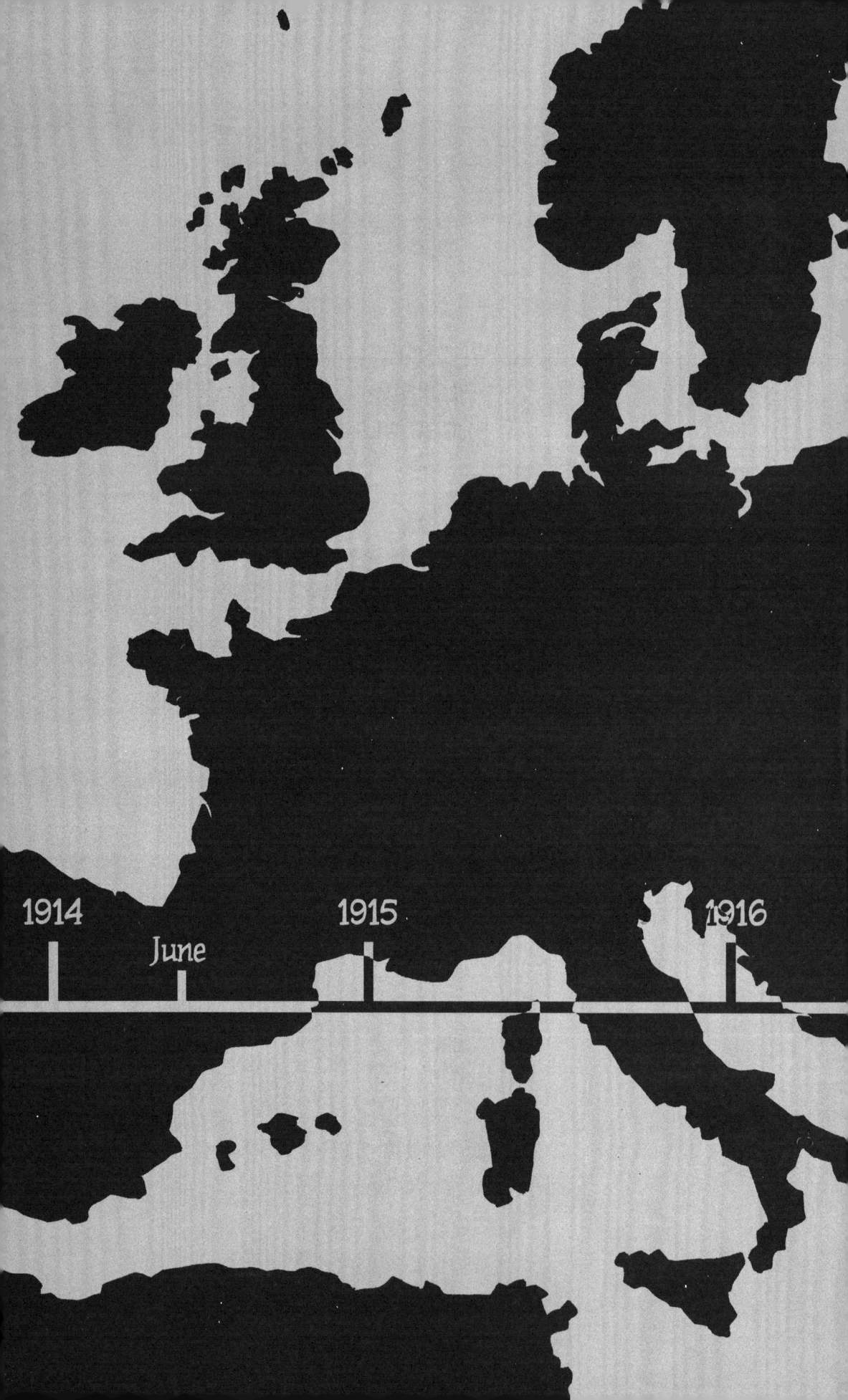

1914

June

1915

1916

Between
1914 and 1918
the First World War
raged across the face
of Europe, forever
changing the World.
Ordinary people
became extra-ordinary
heroes.

1917

1918

November

These are the true
stories of some
of those people...

# INTERNATIONAL ACES

| NATION | : | ACES |
|---|---|---|
| GERMANY | | VON RICHTHOFEN |
| FRANCE | | FONCK |
| CANADA | | BISHOP |
| ENGLAND | | MANNOCK |
| SOUTH AFRICA | | BEAUCHAMP-PROCTO |
| IRELAND | | McELROY |
| AUSTRALIA | | LITTLE |
| BELGIUM | | COPPENS |
| AUSTRO-HUNGARY | | BRUMOWSKI |
| ITALY | | BARACCA |
| U.S.A. | | RICKENBACKER |
| NEW ZEALAND | | CALDWELL |
| RUSSIA | | KOZAKOV |
| INDIA | | LADDIE |

YOUNG PILOTS FROM ACROSS THE WORLD TOOK TO THE
SKIES IN NEWLY INVENTED FLYING MACHINES. LOCKED IN
FEARFUL COMBAT, THEY EARNED 'VICTORIES' WITH EVERY
ENEMY AIRCRAFT THEY SHOT DOWN.

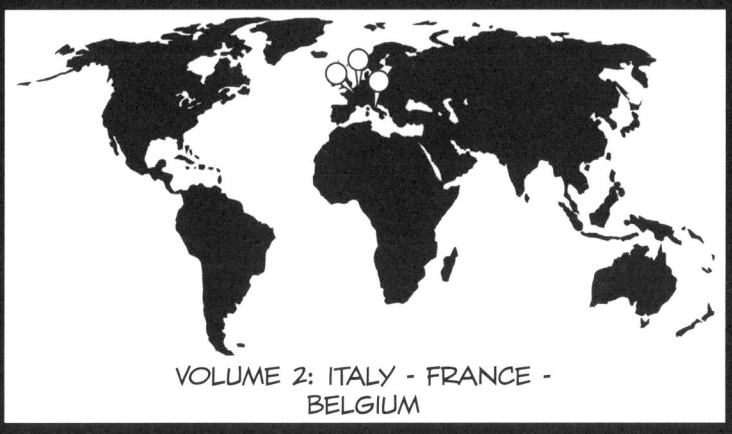

VOLUME 2: ITALY - FRANCE - BELGIUM

| RANK | : VICTORIES |
|---|---|
| RITTMEISTER | 80 |
| CAPITAINE | 75 |
| LIEUTENANT COLONEL | 72 |
| MAJOR | 61 |
| CAPTAIN | 54 |
| CAPTAIN | 47 |
| CAPTAIN | 47 |
| MAJOR | 37 |
| HAUPTMANN | 35 |
| MAGGIORE | 34 |
| CAPTAIN | 26 |
| MAJOR | 25 |
| POLKOVNIK | 20 |
| 2ND LIEUTENANT | 10 |

France — Fonck

England — Mannock

Ireland — McElroy

Belgium — Coppens

Italy — Baracca

New Zealand — Caldwell

India — Laddie

THE TERM 'ACE' WAS USED FOR A PILOT THAT HAD ACHIEVED AT LEAST FIVE CONFIRMED VICTORIES.

Francesco Baracca
Born in Italy
Italian Air Service
34 victories

Italy

Baracca

# LA STAMPA

## L'Italia dichiara la guerra all'Austria

La consegna del passaporto all'Ambasciatore di Francesco Giuseppe
e il richiamo del nostro Ambasciatore a Vienna

La circolare di Sonnino ai nostri rappresentanti all'Estero - L'ultima Nota di
Burian - La guerra per la difesa del buon diritto d'Italia comincia oggi.

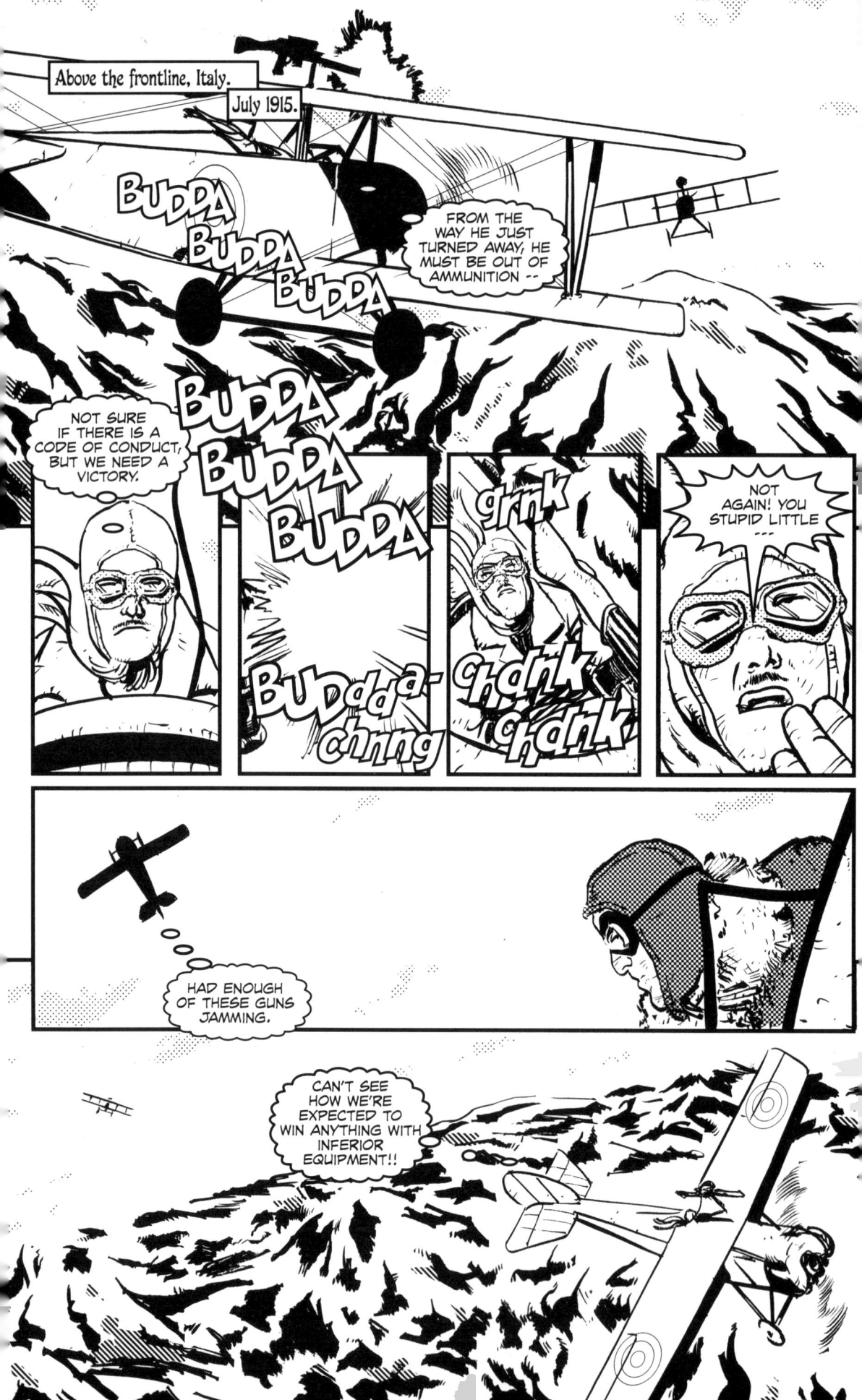

"17th April 1917 – Baracca scores first Italian Victory of the war."

The pilots of 9la Squadron proudly display their freshly painted SPAD VII's for the world to see.

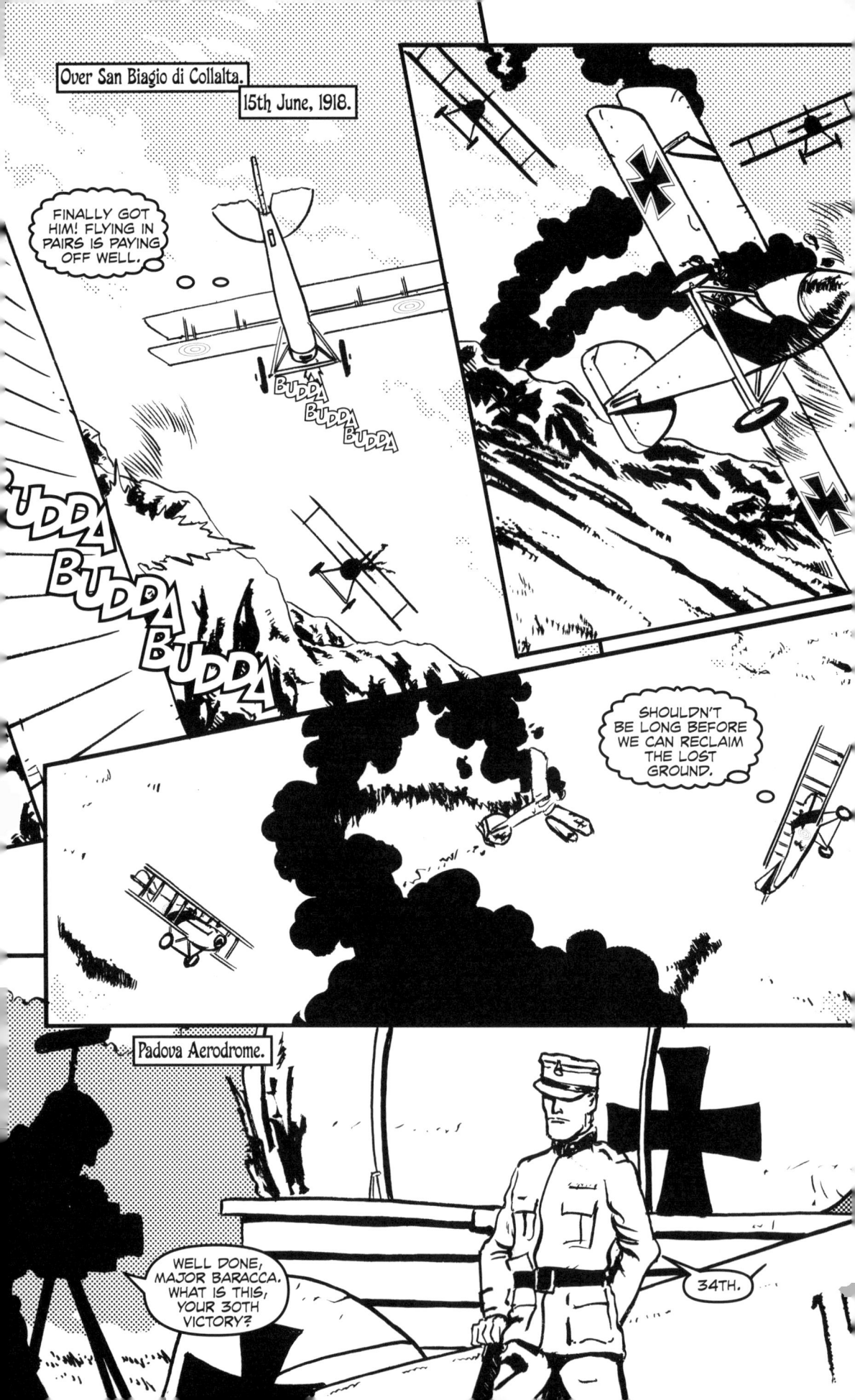

Padova Aerodrome.

GET ME REFUELED AND RELOADED, I'M GOING BACK UP STRAIGHT AWAY.

THEY ARE DEFINITELY ON THE RUN NOW.

FIND A WAY TO STASH SOME EXTRA AMMUNITION TO SAVE US COMING BACK SO OFTEN.

YES, SIR.

YOU SEEN THIS MAJOR?

BULLET'S NEARLY DESTROYED YOUR HEAD REST.

INCH OR TWO OVER AND WE WOULD'VE LOST YOU ON THIS ONE.

DESPERATION IS MAKING THEIR AIM BETTER.

I AM GOING FOR SOME FOOD--

--CALL ME WHEN THE PLANE IS READY TO FLY.

Padova Aerodrome.
19th June, 1918.

REALLY, PICCIO, WE'RE GOING OUT AGAIN?

WE'VE BEEN FLYING ALMOST FOUR DAYS WITHOUT A BREAK!

MAJOR BARACCA HAS DECIDED THAT WE WILL CONTINUE TO GO UP UNTIL OUR WORK IS COMPLETE.

...NO SIR...

OUR MEN IN THE TRENCHES DO NOT COME BACK TO A NICE COSY BED AT THE END OF THE DAY.

MAYBE YOU WOULD LIKE TO TRADE PLACES WITH ONE OF THEM?

EASY, PICCIO.

I AM SURE HE DID NOT MEAN ANY DISRESPECT.

THE LAST FEW DAYS HAVE BEEN RELENTLESS, BUT WE ARE NEAR THE END.

I KNOW THAT YOU ARE ALL TIRED.

OUR BOYS ON THE GROUND HAVE ALMOST BROKEN THROUGH THE ENEMY LINES, BUT THEY NEED THE SUPPORT OF OUR AIR STRIKES.

KEEP YOUR NERVE AND WE WILL SUCCEED.

WITH 34 VICTORIES,
FRANCESCO BARACCA WAS
ITALY'S GREATEST ACE.

END.

Rene Fonck
Born in France
French Air Service
75 victories

France

Fonck

**6TH AUGUST, 1916.**

SORRY TO DISTURB YOU, MAJOR CHASTEL--

--BUT I HAVE BEEN ASKED TO FETCH YOU.

'FETCH ME'? WHAT ARE YOU TALKING ABOUT?

IT'S FONCK, SIR. I THINK YOU SHOULD COME AND SEE.

FONCK, WHAT IS THE MEANING OF THIS?!

YOU KEEP ASKING FOR EVIDENCE, MAJOR--

--WELL, HERE IT IS.

I GOT THIS DOWN WITHOUT USING ANY WEAPONS WHATSOEVER.

WHO ELSE CAN GO, UNARMED, AGAINST AN ENEMY PLANE, THAT IS FULLY ARMED--

--AND FORCE IT TO THE GROUND?

HOW MANY OF YOUR FIGHTER PILOTS CAN DO THAT?

HOW MANY, MAJOR?

AM I NOT THE GREATEST?

YOU ARE AN ARROGANT FOOL.

AM I NOT THE GREATEST?

AM I NOT THE GREATEST?!

**15 APRIL, 1917. ST POL-SUR-MER.**

AERODROME OF THE FAMOUS GROUP DE COMBAT 12. 'LES CIGOGNES'

--AND IF YOU'LL COME WITH ME, ADJUTANT FONCK--

I'LL SHOW YOU TO YOUR NEW BARRACKS.

THANK YOU...

JUST CALL ME 'GRUE', SIR.

THANK YOU, GRUE.

WHAT IS GOING ON OVER THERE?

OH THAT'S JUST GEORGES GUYNEMER, SIR.

I BELIEVE THAT HE'S JUST BEEN GIVEN A NEW PLANE.

QUITE A BEAUTY FROM WHAT I HEAR.

I SUPPOSE THE BEST PILOT SHOULD GET THE BEST PLANE.

COULDN'T AGREE MORE.

SO JUST HOW MANY VICTORIES ARE YOU GOING TO GET WITH THIS, GUYNEMER?

OH, AT LEAST FIFTY!

YOU CARRY ON LIKE THAT AND THERE WON'T BE ANY LEFT FOR THE REST OF US.

HA HA HA HA HA HA HA

THE GERMANS ARE KEEN TO ENTERTAIN US --

-- I'M SURE THERE WILL STILL BE PLENTY TO GO AROUND.

HELLO, WHO DO WE HAVE HERE?

JUST ADMIRING YOUR PLANE, MONSIEUR GUYNEMER. I USE --

IF YOU WISH TO ADDRESS ME, MONSIEUR, THE RANK IS CAPTAIN.

SORRY, CAPTAIN. MY NAME IS FONCK. ADJUTANT RENE FONCK.

I USED TO BE AN ENGINEER. I WAS JU--

THAT'S VERY NICE, BUT AS THIS PLANE IS VERY NEW AND VERY EXPENSIVE, I WOULD PREFER IF YOU WERE TO STEP AWAY.

I WAS JUST --

I WOULD ASSUME, ADJUTANT, THAT AS YOU ARE NEW HERE, YOU HAVE SOME UNPACKING TO DO.

NO DOUBT WE WILL SPEAK AGAIN.

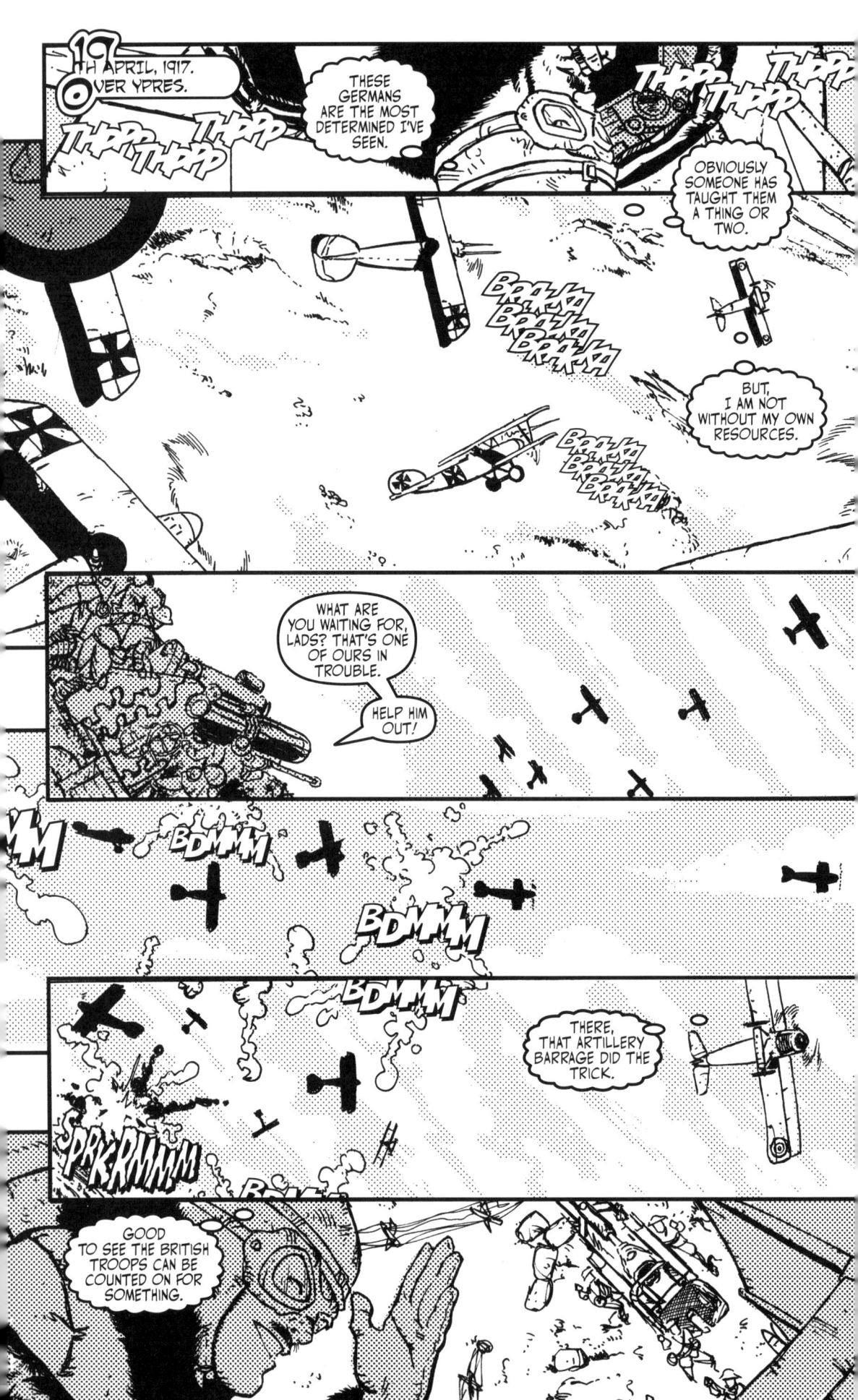

WHY IS THAT FOOL LOOKING AT ME?!

NOTHING I C -- WHAT'S THAT?!

SPEAKING OF FOOLS. ALMOST GOT HIT BY HIS FALLING PLANE.

WELL, IN OR OUT OF THE PLANE HE WOULDN'T HAVE SURVIVED.

STILL, I SUPPOSE THERE ARE BETTER WAYS TO GO.

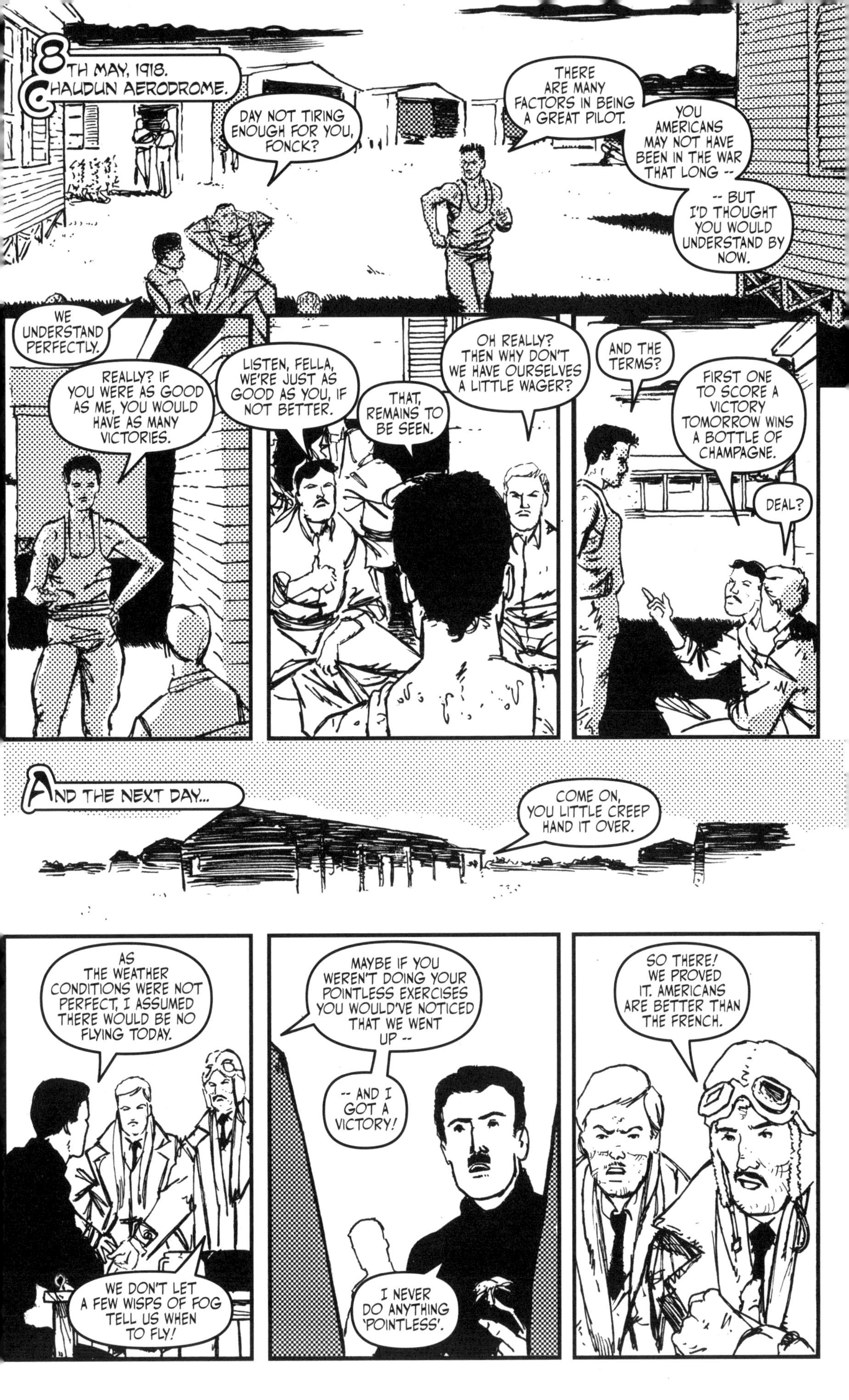

8TH MAY, 1918. CHAUDUN AERODROME.

DAY NOT TIRING ENOUGH FOR YOU, FONCK?

THERE ARE MANY FACTORS IN BEING A GREAT PILOT.

YOU AMERICANS MAY NOT HAVE BEEN IN THE WAR THAT LONG --

-- BUT I'D THOUGHT YOU WOULD UNDERSTAND BY NOW.

WE UNDERSTAND PERFECTLY.

REALLY? IF YOU WERE AS GOOD AS ME, YOU WOULD HAVE AS MANY VICTORIES.

LISTEN, FELLA, WE'RE JUST AS GOOD AS YOU, IF NOT BETTER.

THAT REMAINS TO BE SEEN.

OH REALLY? THEN WHY DON'T WE HAVE OURSELVES A LITTLE WAGER?

AND THE TERMS?

FIRST ONE TO SCORE A VICTORY TOMORROW WINS A BOTTLE OF CHAMPAGNE.

DEAL?

AND THE NEXT DAY...

COME ON, YOU LITTLE CREEP HAND IT OVER.

AS THE WEATHER CONDITIONS WERE NOT PERFECT, I ASSUMED THERE WOULD BE NO FLYING TODAY.

WE DON'T LET A FEW WISPS OF FOG TELL US WHEN TO FLY!

MAYBE IF YOU WEREN'T DOING YOUR POINTLESS EXERCISES YOU WOULD'VE NOTICED THAT WE WENT UP --

-- AND I GOT A VICTORY!

I NEVER DO ANYTHING 'POINTLESS'.

SO THERE! WE PROVED IT. AMERICANS ARE BETTER THAN THE FRENCH.

FONCK SURVIVED THE WAR AND PUBLISHED HIS MEMOIRS, 'MES COMBATS' IN 1920.

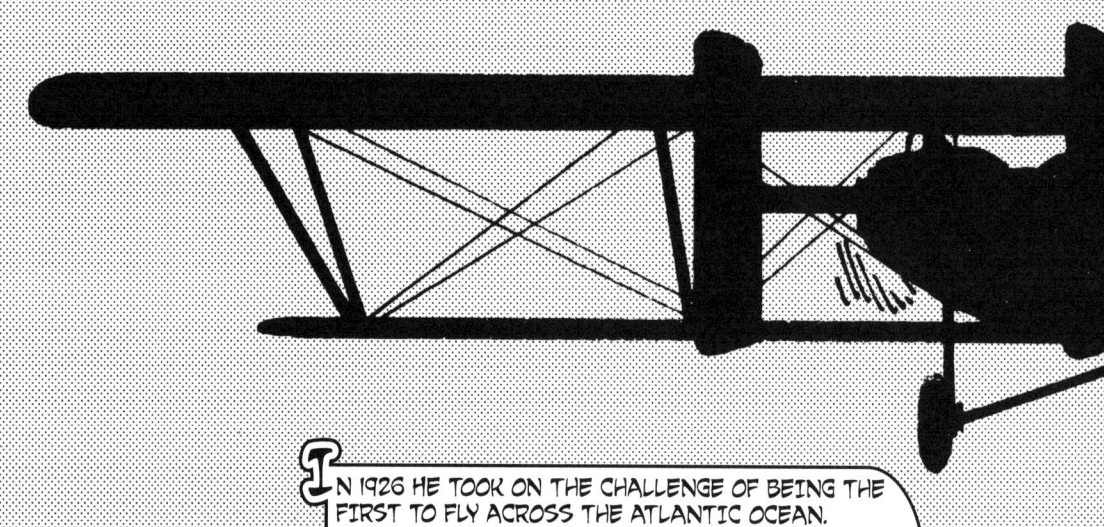

IN 1926 HE TOOK ON THE CHALLENGE OF BEING THE FIRST TO FLY ACROSS THE ATLANTIC OCEAN. UNFORTUNATELY HIS HUGE S.35 PLANE CRASHED DURING TAKEOFF. FONCK RECOVERED, BUT IT WAS AN AMERICAN, CHARLES LINDENBURGH, WHO WON THE FIRST, NON-STOP, SOLO TRANS-ATLANTIC PRIZE IN 1927.

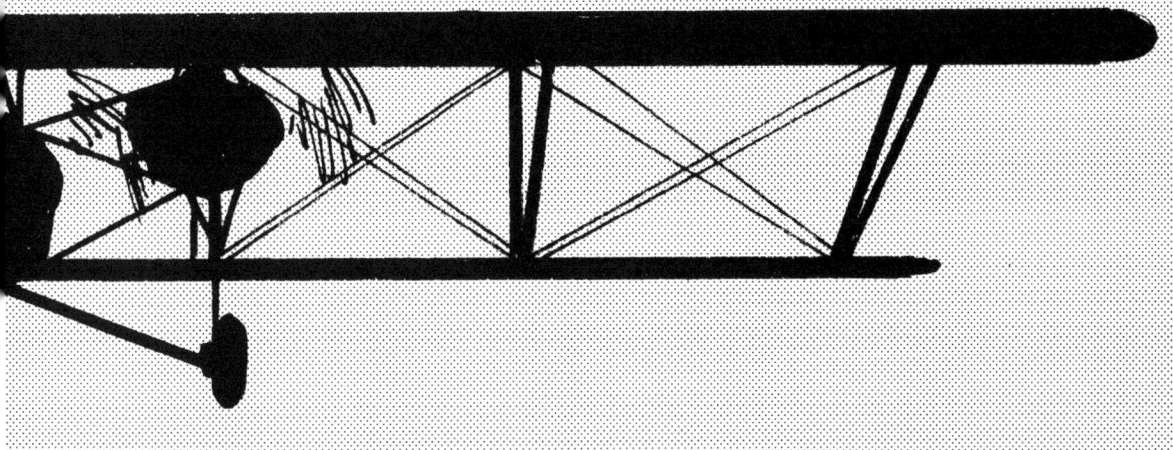

WITH 75 VICTORIES, RENE FONCK WAS FRANCE'S GREATEST ACE.

END.

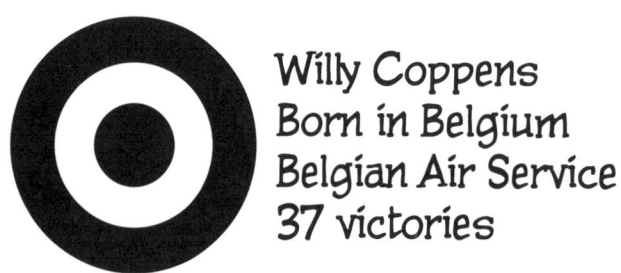

Willy Coppens
Born in Belgium
Belgian Air Service
37 victories

Belgium

Coppens

High above the German frontline, Willy Coppens flies his Nieuport 17 to it's limits as he heads into his home country of Belgium.

The bombardment continues until long after midnight.

Trapped, the Belgium troops huddle together in the trenches.

As dawn arrives, they wait in dread for the next wave of attacks.

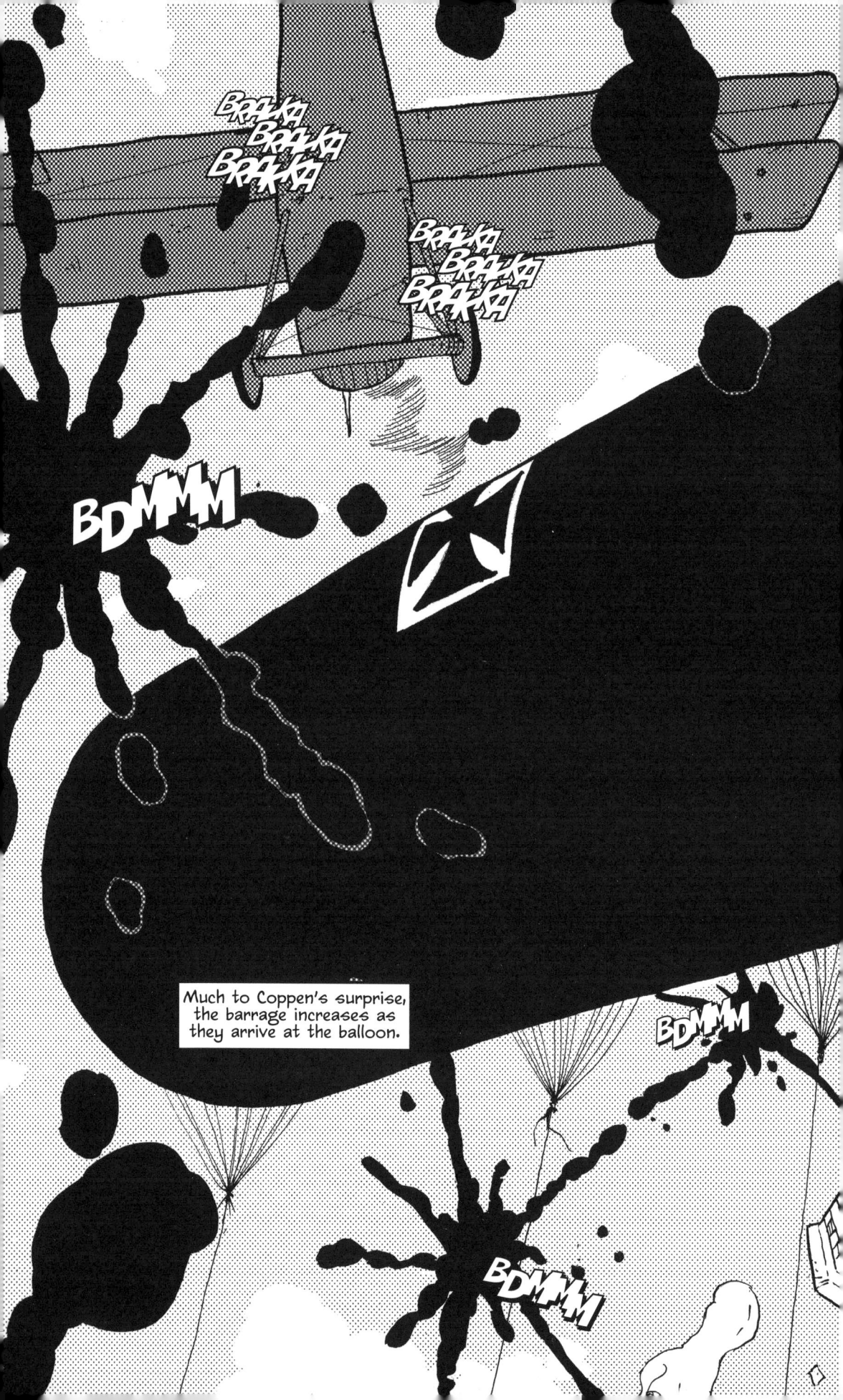

Much to Coppen's surprise, the barrage increases as they arrive at the balloon.

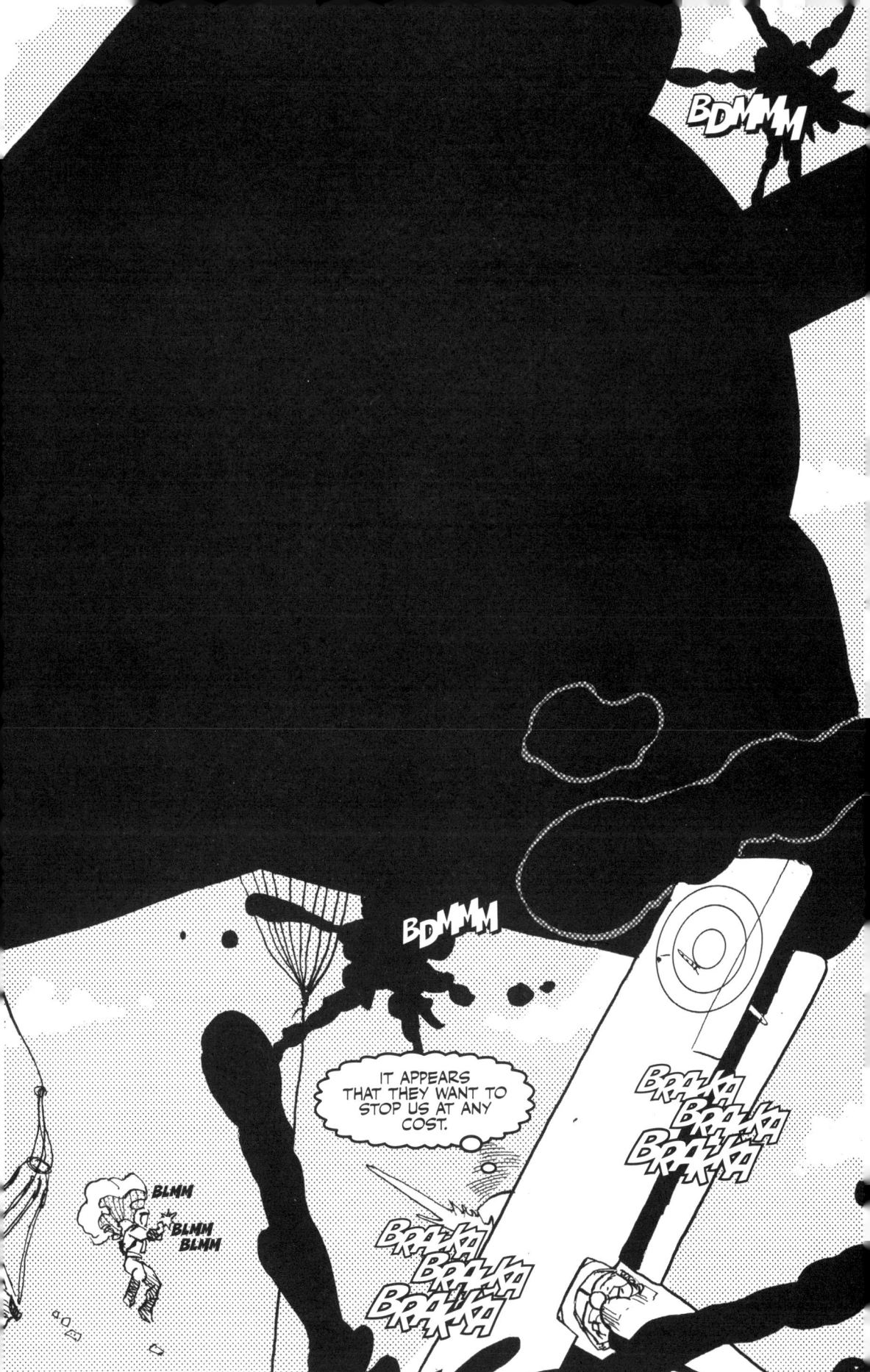

BALLOON FEELS LIKE IT'S STARTING TO COLLAPSE --
-- WONDER WHAT WILL HAPPEN NOW...
WELL, ASK A STUPID QUESTION...
AT LEAST I'M OFF THE BALLOON --
-- NOW TO GET THE RIGHT WAY UP.

Coppens continued his
successful balloons attacks
until he was wounded on
14th October 1918.
Although he made it back to
the allied lines, his left leg
needed to be amputated.

His adventurous spirit was
undiminished and in 1928,
whilst wearing a prosthetic
leg, Coppens set a new
parachute record, jumping
from an altitude of 19,700
feet.

With 37 victories, Willy Coppens
was Belgium's greatest ace.

END.

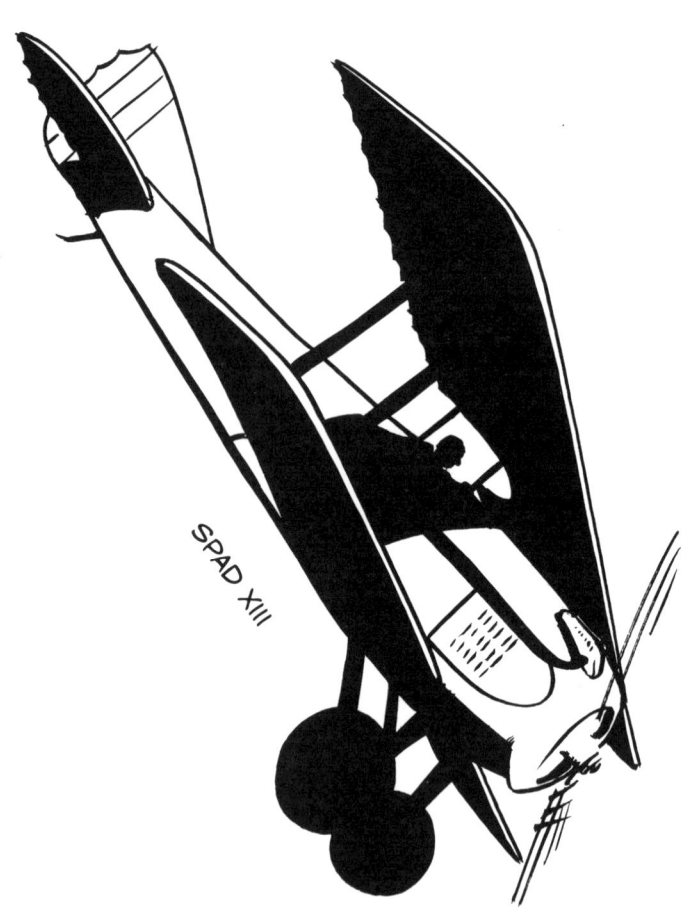

SPAD XIII

At 11am
on 11th November 1918, the
First World War was
over.

Each year, at the
11th Hour, of the 11th Day, of the 11th Month
we pay tribute to those
who fought during this, and
more recent, wars.

We will always remember them.

First World War
Centenary

# INTERNATIONAL ACES
## FIRST WORLD WAR SERIES

## Volume One
The Series starts with Aces from India, Ireland and England.

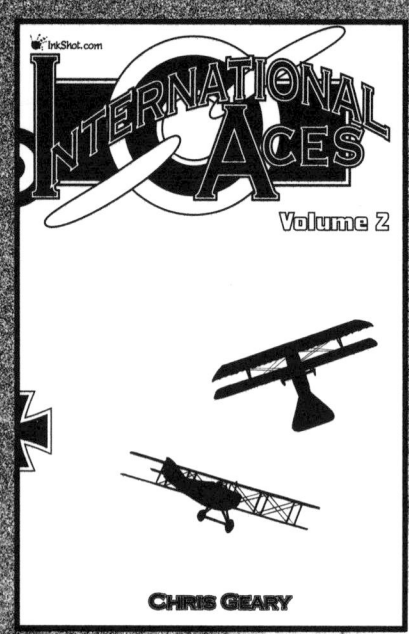

## Volume Two
Includes Aces from Italy, France and Belgium.

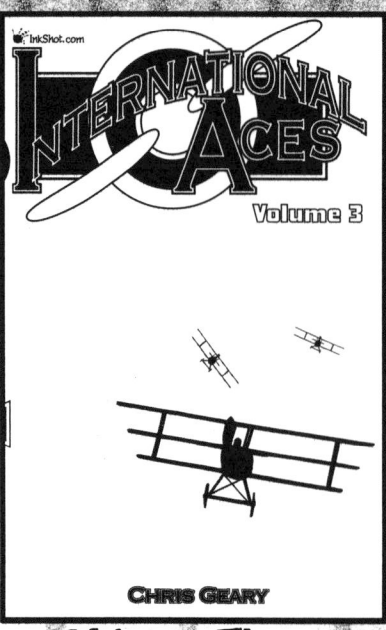

## Volume Three
Features Aces from Russia, Germany and Austro-Hungary.

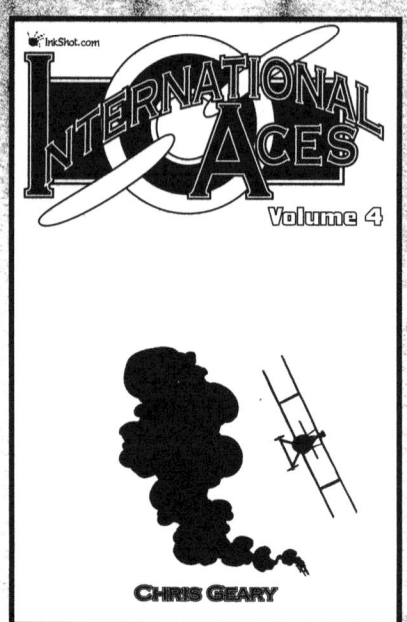

## Volume Four
Includes Aces from Canada, South Africa, Australia, New Zealand and The United States.